First Phrases from Around the World

Everyday Russian

Tricia Hoffman

Little Mitchie
an imprint of Mitchell Lane

CREATING YOUNG NONFICTION READERS

Little Mitchie books spark curiosity and support early nonfiction reading for students in Grades 2-3. Designed to build vocabulary, support second language learners, and prepare readers for middle-grade content, each book includes helpful tips for parents and educators to build confidence and deepen understanding of the world.

TIPS FOR READING NONFICTION WITH BEGINNING READERS

Talk about Nonfiction

Begin by explaining that nonfiction books give us information that is true. The book will be organized around a specific topic or idea, and we may learn new facts through reading.

Look at the Parts

Most nonfiction books have helpful features. Our *Little Mitchie* titles include color photographs and graphic aids, a table of contents, a glossary, and an index. Share the purpose of these features with your reader.

Color Photos and Graphic Aids

A lot of information can be found by "reading" photos, charts, maps, and other graphic aids found within nonfiction texts. Help your reader learn more about the different ways information can be displayed.

Table of Contents

Located at the front of the book, this list shows the big ideas within the text and the page numbers where they can be found.

Index

Located at the back of the book, an index is an alphabetical list of topics and the page numbers where they can be found.

With a little help and guidance about reading nonfiction, you can feel good about introducing a young reader to the world of *Little Mitchie* nonfiction books.

Little Mitchie is an imprint of:

Mitchell Lane
PUBLISHERS

2001 SW 31st Avenue
Hallandale, FL 33009
mitchelllanepub.com

First Edition, 2027.

Author: Tricia Hoffman
Designer: Kathy Walsh
Editor: Tricia Hoffman

Library of Congress Cataloging-in-Publication Data
Title: Everyday Russian / by Tricia Hoffman

Description: Hallandale, FL :
Mitchell Lane Publishers, [2027]

Identifiers:
Library bound ISBN: 979-8-89260-913-5
Paperback ISBN: 979-8-90145-064-2
eBook ISBN: 979-8-90145-023-9

Library of Congress Control Number: 2026931266

PHOTO CREDITS: Cover and Title pg: iukhym_vova, smile3377; Doodle Art: devitaayu, FourLeafLover, wanchana, veekicl, Rizky, mhatzapa, Kebon doodle, Asyam Design, piixypeach, syoko: istock: background, rica nohara; p 4, Vagengeim, Supertrooper, Ixepop; p 5, Dragana Gordic; p 6, Mabuka, Andrey Arkusha; p 7, Eric Isselee, Pixel-Shot; p 9, ViDI Studio; p 10, Roman Chazov, PeopleImages, Volodymyr TVERDOKHLIB; p 11, Yuliya D'yakova; p 12, BAZA Production, Chiociolla, Chase D'animulls, BongoStock; p 13, Bet_Noire, Volodymyr TVERDOKHLIB; p 14, NataliaBiruk, pics five, Albina Gavrilovic; p 15, SviatlanaLaza, People Images; p 16, PeopleImages, Volodymyr TVERDOKHLIB, FamVeld; p 17, Sorapop Udomsri; p 18, Elena Rostunova, SSTK 4K, BearFotos; p 19, Synthetic Messiah, BearFotos; p 20, Dasha Trofimova, PicMy, Inside Creative House; p 21, New Africa, Ira Lichi, New Africa, DROBOT VIKTORIIA, New Africa; p 22, Pixel-Shot, Di Studio, New Africa; p 23, New Africa

Table of Contents

This Is Me

Mne vosem' let.

I am eight years old.

Menya zovut Aleksandr.

My name is Aleksandr.

Eto ya

odin
one

dva
two

tri
three

chetyre
four

pyat'
five

shest'
six

sem'
seven

vosem'
eight

devyat'
nine

desyat'
ten

People and Pets

Ya zhivu so svoyey sem'yey.

I live with my family.

brat
brother

otets
father

sestra
sister

mat'
mother

Lyudi i domashniye zhivotnyye

U menya yest' domashniye zhivotnyye.

I have pets.

Today

Segodnya voskresen'ye.

Today is Sunday.

voskresen'ye
Sunday

ponedel'nik
Monday

vtornik
Tuesday

sreda
Wednesday

chetverg
Thursday

pyatnitsa
Friday

subbota
Saturday

Seychas iyun'.

The month is June.

yanvar' . . . . January
fevral' . . . . February
mart . . . . March
aprel'. . . . . April
mai . . . . May
iyun' . . . . June
iyul' . . . . July
avgust . . . . August
sentyabr' . . . . September
oktyabr' . . . . . October
noyabr'. . . . . . November
dekabr' . . . . . . December

Segodnya

Na ulitse solnechno.

It is sunny outside.

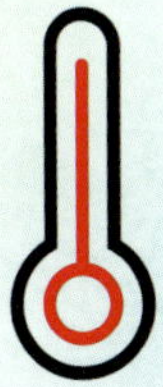

zharko

hot

kholodno

cold

dozhdlivo

rainy

vetreno

windy

Morning

Dobroye utro!

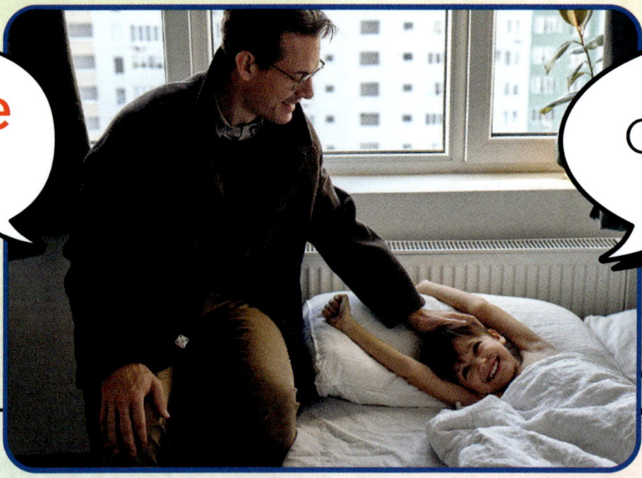

Good morning!

Ya raschesyvayu volosy.

I comb my hair.

Ya chishchu zuby.

I brush my teeth.

Utro

Ya noshu zholtuyu shlyapu.

I wear a yellow hat.

oranzhevyy orange	zheltyy yellow	siniy blue	zelyonyy green
fioletovyy purple	krasnyy red	rozovyy pink	
chernyy black	belyy white		

Breakfast

Ya khochu na zavtrak khlop'ya, pozhaluysta.

I want cereal for breakfast, please.

tost
toast

apel'sinovyy sok
orange juice

bekon
bacon

yaytso
egg

Zavtrak

Avtobus pribyl.
Pora yekhat'!

The bus is here.
It is time to go!

shkol'nyy avtobus
school bus

ryukzak
backpack

School

Ya khozhu v shkolu.

I go to school.

Ya chitayu.

I read.

Ya zanimayus' matematikoy.

I do math.

Shkola

Mne nuzhna pomoshch'.

I need help.

uchitel'
teacher

rabochiy stol
desk

Mozhno mne skhodit' v tualet?

May I go to the bathroom?

Time to Play

Ty poigrayesh' so mnoy?

Will you play with me?

Da!

Yes!

Ya begayu.
I run.

Ya kachayus'.
I swing.

Vremya igrat'

Ya brosayu myach.

I throw a ball.

glaza
eyes

ushi
ears

rot
mouth

rubashka
shirt

ruka
arm

Neighborhood

Ya zhivu v zhilom rayone.

I live in a neighborhood.

Ya mashu rukoy svoyemu drugu.

I wave to my friend.

Ya idu v magazin.

I go to the store.

Rayon

Skol'ko eto stoit?

How much does this cost?

derevo
tree

stena
wall

trava
grass

voda
water

Dinner

Da, pozhaluysta.
Yes, please.

Net, spasibo.
No, thank you.

Uzhin

Mne nravitsya russkaya kukhnya.
I like Russian food.

syrniki
pancakes

borscht
beet soup

pelmeni
dumplings

pirozhki
pastries

Mne nravitsya amerikanskaya yeda.
I like American food.

sendvich
sandwich

yabloko
apple

Night

Ya noshu pizhamu.

I wear pajamas.

Ya idu spat'.

I go to bed.

Ya zakryvayu glaza.

I close my eyes.

Noch'

podushka
pillow

odeyalo
blanket

Index

About Russian

Russian is the seventh most common language in the world. About 260 million people speak Russian as either a first or second language. The top three countries where Russian is spoken are Russia, Ukraine, and Belarus. Russian is the official language of four countries in Europe and Asia, including Russia, Belarus, Kazakhstan, and Kyrgyzstan. One unique thing about this language is that there are no native Russian words that begin with the letter *a*. These words were borrowed from other languages such as French or German.